Waiting for Insanity Clause

poems by

Gary Walton

Finishing Line Press
Georgetown, Kentucky

Waiting for Insanity Clause

Copyright © 2017 by Gary Walton
ISBN 978-1-63534-110-2 First Edition
All rights reserved under International and Pan-American Copyright Conventions. No part of this book may be reproduced in any manner whatsoever without written permission from the publisher, except in the case of brief quotations embodied in critical articles and reviews.

ACKNOWLEDGMENTS

Some of the poems in this collection first appeared in *For A Better World: Poems and Drawings on Peace and Justice by Greater Cincinnati Artists, 2011, 2012, 2013, 2014, 2015, 2016; Levure litteraire, International Magazine for Information and Cultural Education; AEQAI; meTaDada* and *California Quarterly*. The author wishes to thank the editors of these publications for printing his work.

Publisher: Leah Maines

Editor: Christen Kincaid

Front Cover Design: Chuck Feltner (from an original photo
 by Kathy Otto)

Back Cover Design: Chuck Feltner (from an original
 drawing by Brandon Otto)

Author Photo: from Gary Walton collection

Printed in the USA on acid-free paper.
Order online: www.finishinglinepress.com
 also available on amazon.com

Author inquiries and mail orders:
Finishing Line Press
P. O. Box 1626
Georgetown, Kentucky 40324
U. S. A.

Table of Contents

Melissa Moon at Breakfast 1

Here in Garbageland© 3

Doing the Chores: Sex and Laundry 5

Afterwards 7

Complaining to Death 8

Waiting for Insanity Clause 10

The Ghosts of Christmas 11

The Filthy Snow 12

Angela 15

Sojourners 16

Fear and Loathing: the Last Election 18

Cut to: Slow Dissolve 20

The Doomsday Clock 21

Life in Beta 23

Filling my Former Plenum 24

The Peach 25

Seated in the Restaurant 27

*To: Bev and Charley; Kathy and Timel—
As always....*

"What youthful mother, shape upon her lap...
Would think her son, did she but see that shape
With sixty or more winters on its head,
A compensation for the pang of birth,
Or the uncertainty of his setting forth?"
—W. B. Yeats, "Among School Children"

"Round and round we spin, with feet of lead and wings of tin."
—Kurt Vonnegut, "Cat's Cradle"

"Dear Editor.
I am 8 years old. Some of my little friends say there is not a Santa Claus....
Please tell me the truth; is there a Santa Clause?
Signed
Virginia O'Hanlon
NYC

Virginia, your little friends are wrong. They have been affected by the skepticism of a skeptical age....All minds, Virginia whether they be men's or children's, are little. In this great universe of ours man is a mere insect, an ant, in his intellect, as compared with the boundless world about him, as measured by the intelligence capable of grasping the whole of truth and knowledge."
—letter to the editor (and response),
New York Sun, 1897

"You can't fool me—there ain't no sanity clause...."
—Chico, *A Night at the Opera*

Melissa Moon at Breakfast

"You can't depend on other people
For your happiness," Melissa Moon said,
Shifting in her chair, arranging her paisley
Kimono, all the while nibbling on a wedge

Of buttered toast and raspberry marmalade.
"I'm simply tired of mourning for my
Country, writing eulogies for my friends—
And feeling sorry for myself….I'm not

Saying one needs to be a lone wolf.
A pack has its uses, especially if you
Are hungry"—here she popped a plump
Strawberry into her mouth and let a bit

Of the red juice ooze from the corners
Of her lips—"No, one needs to think of
The butterfly, a Monarch perhaps, rising
Alone on summer thermals, head tilted

Toward the sun, defiant of gravity and all
Opinion, up and up toward—where?—
Argentina?—no. Nirvana?—a bit presumptuous,
Perhaps—but at least, tomorrow—of course, one

Need not be so grand, at all. How about a
Single rose bush, beside a house, a modest
House, a shack, in fact—one can bloom in the
Most humble of settings…." Here she stopped;

A wedge of melon pinioned on a fork, she
Brandished like a sword. She stood up,
As if in mild alarm, and declared, "My God,
I need a pencil—the time has come! I must

Write something down...." With that, she
Twirled and fluttered and fled the room
Like a flag unfurling. Soon the typewriter
Was clacking away in the next room.

The day had begun....

Here in Garbageland©

The rides are made from Peckerwood
Throwaways, like this Ferris wheel here
Fashioned from blood and bone, and
Billions of bent beer cans, bolted and

Pinned with toxic syringes, glued with
Abandoned dreams frozen in perpetual
Plastic wrap, insulated from the ground
By perfectly formed rhetorical phrases like

The kind found in bathroom stalls or
Scratched indelibly in the sacred wood
Of church pews and altars or thrown
Carelessly from the most pious of pulpits—

The wheel turns like an escapement lit
By incandescent bulbs and the runway
Flashes blue and red, then black and blue
And the cotton candy swirls come with

Insulin pills to ward off diabetic shock—
All the while, we sing and sing and shout
At the video screen which continually
Reminds us that hope is a product patented

By Bristol-Meyers and sold in sacks like peanuts
To sightless elephants. Tickets must be
Purchased early, not to beat the rush, but
To confound the summer tornadoes, who

Always seem to know how to call the tunes
Even if it's the last one you will ever
Hear—but it's a ride you'll never forget to
Remember and the roustabouts and Chinese

Gaffers full of viridian tattoos of teardrops
And hermetic Sanskrit, laugh and laugh
Here at the summer fair, the carnival
Just at the edge of town.

Doing the Chores: Sex and Laundry

It is Tuesday, a weekday, a
    Weak day, cloudy and not the

Sabbath, a workday and alas
    Laundry day, and she feels as if

She has just washed the clothes,
    Yesterday,

But that bit of impedimenta was
    Last Monday already and the days

Whiz by like amusement park *divertissements*,
    Blurring images and faces as in a

House of mirrors made of foil or
    Like the skyline from atop a tilt-

o-whirl, and she wonders what the
    World will be like at the end of

The ride when the gears grind
    To a full stop—and she imagines

An old hag on a gurney covered
    In a dull green cotton gown, a

Pale preview of her own final cerements,
    And she thinks, "I will be that she,

Looking over the edge at what there
Is to see and wondering if Freud

Was right, if it all, all of 'it,' was about
    sex—though sometimes

It was hidden in brute disguises,
Sometimes in subtle sentimental

Costumes to veil the true pedestrian
Character of the ultimate affair—."

How daunting to realize all of the
Music, dancing, high-minded rhetoric,

Much less the dinners, the intrigues,
The subterfuges, were merely to get the

Next generation born—are we, then, just so many
Rutting fools, clowns to nature, harlequins

Stumbling along a prescribed quotidian sojourn?
Such paltry musing is scant comfort

When she must dip her hands in
The frothy water, to once again squeeze

Out the dirt, to refresh the act for
One more performance. Then, for an

Instant, she wishes she could dive in the tub
    And drown her past, wash her worries

Like the Kajol from her eyes, wipe her mind
    Clean like lipstick from his shirt collar

And rise again as if baptized into a world
    Made anew: bleached white and wrinkle free.

Afterwards

Since he's gone,
She only makes half the bed;
The other remains pristine, if not
Serene, untouched, unsullied,
Though her patch is sullen
Territory, confused, tortured
And unforgiving;

In the closet, his clothes
Hang like bitter memories,
But she can't bear to throw
Them out, although a few
Have been torn by hands
Filled with anger and
Frustration—some simply
Wipe tears when she can't
Resist holding the cloth
Up to her nose to smell
The linger of his aftershave;

This is what life has come to,
Living in these margins, like
Abandoned punctuation in a
Forgotten biography or some
Sentimental novel—this
Is the price one pays for love:
Loving too hard for too long—
God, if he were here now,
She'd kill him for leaving.

Complaining to Death
> *"By the way—you look fantastic in your boots of Chinese plastic."*
> —Chrissy Hynde

Melissa Moon sat down for the interview
    In a small café located in an indifferent
        Part of town—already Christmas displays

Had invaded the shelves of stores though
    It was still late October—"Should one say
        Merry Christmas…" Ms. Moon opined while

Lighting up a black and brown twisted cheroot
    To the frowns of slack-faced on-lookers, "when
        One hasn't even begun to Trick-or-treat? My

God, Thanksgiving! Think of that!" she said,
    As she forced blue-gray smoke through her
        Pursed lips making an ephemeral filigree in

The still air—then after ordering a soup and
    Campari with ice, the author looked around
        At the tables and then the street with dismay.

"I think complaining has become
    My métier," she said, without blinking, "a
        Way of being in the world—not much we can

Do to change anything, though—and even if
    We could change the government or even
        People's minds there is still death to contend

With—and…," she said sighing, "worse
    Decrepitude—that slow painful waiting and
        Wasting away into superfluity and oblivion…."

Here she stopped and strummed her fingers
    On the Formica table top as if pausing for
        A distant tune to return to her memory—

"...and now look," she said, pointing with
    The burning tip of her tiny cigar, "my soup
        Is cold and my ice has melted—it's maddening

To be constantly victimized by this incessant
    Entropy—when, Mon Cher, is enough, finally, *Enough!*"
        "Merry Christmas," she said to one

Of the carved pumpkins sitting in the window,
    As she stood up and walked briskly to the
        Sidewalk, leaving her companion completely

Nonplussed watching the heels of her boots strike
    The concrete with a delicate feminine defiance
        That sent tiny sparks into the growing dusk,

Barely illuminating that delicate moment
    Before the streetlights blink on and
        The city's mood shifts from taupe to mauve.

Waiting for Insanity Clause

Today is Christmas Eve
And I think I will clean my
Toilet, perhaps dust my socks

And underwear and other personal
Ornaments too private to be hung
On the public mantel to be stuffed

With Holiday cheer. Later, I might
Wrap what's left of my youth and
Place it beneath the tree, a gift I

Can no longer keep nor one I am
Able to give to another—tonight I
Will wander the streets in search of

Lazarus and Diogenes to hear what
They might have to tell me—alas, I
Am not optimistic: I am skeptical of all

Information received from third parties;
When I tire, I think I will come home,
Crawl under the covers and listen

For sleigh bells and tiny hooves—
A childish act, I know—but I yearn
For immortal illusion to bring the

Morning, not for fulfillment or wonder,
That would be too much here at the edge
Of dawn—but perhaps the morning could

Bring a modest gift, even if it's just
A brief, if chastened
Smile.

The Ghosts of Christmas

It is Christmas day and
She is alone—hung over;
There is no tree, no lights,
No garish paper—
Only silence, except for the
Intermittent galumph of the furnace fan;

Her project today is to pump
Air into her tires—not an easy
Task in America on such a
Special day when nothing is open
Except Chinese restaurants and
The gaping wounds of the
Annual annunciation of recrimination—

Besides, she wants to be ready for
Marley's ghost or the imperfect
Shades of defunct friends and family
Who might stop by uninvited
But whose memory might find
A kind of welcome, none the less—
They could all climb into her car
With a cracked bottle of rye and
Cruise around the neighborhood,
Hooting at the hoarfrosted windows and
Haloed, colored lights, haunting the
Streets, pretending they were a
Currier and Ives card sent to
Brighten up someone else's day—

At least, that was the plan,
If she could just find her
Car keys and the will to open
The garage door
Once the motor is running—

The Filthy Snow

Today, the snow is falling
    Heavily, like asbestos from
        A demolition site—think of the ones

In Detroit whose bones are picked
    Apart and shipped overseas
        While the workers stand idly by,

Weeping; huge piles smother the
    Brown winter grass, hide the red
        Rust on the used Japanese cars

Abandoned along the city street.
    School has been cancelled; the
        Roads impassable; our town is stuck

In sudden climactic dysfunction.
    Thus, I am home, stymied in my
        Own forward movement, observing

The world from behind my blinds,
    Remembering a similar storm
        Long ago when I was away from

Home, on the road, a musician,
    Traveling with a famous doo-wop band
        Whose legacy of hit recordings and film

Kept them working long after their
    Moment had passed—still, show
        Business, like each newly falling

Flake, held a certain delight in its
    Sheer novelty, bright and slick and
        Cool, each footfall making an imprint

And progress could be measured
>Through the receding tumbled drifts
>>And sudden ruffling gusts of fortune—

In Montreal during a blizzard,
>My French was as bad as the weather;
>>*Mon Dieu! Quel imbécile j'étais ignorante;*

In that very European, North American city
>Men and Women wore matching full-length
>>Furs and hats of mink, drank Cognac in snifters;

Some bathed in a heated pool, uncovered,
>Observing the stars on the hotel roof,
>>Steam rising like pure souls to heaven

But their bodies luxuriated in the soft
>Intoxication of the mist—what was weather
>>To a people so full of *joie de vivre?*

Life was grand and unsullied
>Like *la nouvelle neige* that
>>Now engulfs my garden Hotei Buddah;

But I cannot keep that pristine vision—
>Soon, I find my mind slipping like a
>>Foolish pedestrian on an icy sidewalk

Into an imprecise allusion to Jimmy
>Joyce's "Dead" and I too feel the clutch
>>Of vague dread as the flakes fall through

The universe covering every leaf and
>Branch and blade and grain of asphalt
>>As they descend like the last end of us all;

And even now, as I watch, the virgin
    Ice is already collecting bits of black
        Ash and motes of other dark confetti

Confirming that, without warning, like
    A sudden Nor'easter, we too will be
        Quieted under the weight of the

Filthy, filthy, snow.

Angela

Angela could do cartwheels
    Into a fan;
She practiced days and days
    Without end,
Wearing her scars and bruises
    Like a Martyr;
One morning a shiny chrome blade
    Sliced off her head;
Then, Angela was an artist,
    Perhaps the only one
Our little town had even seen
    (That we can remember);
We appreciated her sacrifice—
    Well, some of us did;
Someone even placed the bloody fan
    Into a gallery
Beside a wall in a long slender room
    Next to a garden;
People strolled by to and fro
    Most were oblivious;
A few expressed disgust
    And exited quickly
Hiding the children's eyes,
    Pulling away their own
When they realized what
    They were exposed to;
Angela would be pleased
    At least, I think so,
But on the other hand
    Perhaps she would not;
It's so hard to tell such Sturm and
    Drang, n'est pas?
Since Angela is not here to say;
    There's just the fan.

Sojourners
"The Singularity is Near...."
—Ray Kurzweil, 2005

They say the singularity
    Will occur sometime around 2045
        When the machines will become
            Self-conscious, not like a single

Teenage boy with two terrible feet
    And a face full of violent acne
        Forced by his mother into a
            Room full of young ladies, themselves

Blossoming in precocious pubescent regalia,
    Trying desperately to learn
        To dance the waltz—one, two, three;
            No, the computer awakening will be

More basic—like the time a toddler
    Learns she is not the cat, or that she
        Likes strawberry but not double chocolate
            Chunk ice cream, even if it has heliotrope

Sprinkles and mauve whipped topping,
    Not even with a cherry at its very tippy-top—
        When "I" and "me" become much
            More than binary lines of code

To those digital doyens and the
    Word "morning" becomes a time and
        A place and a present, a "now";
            Will we bone and meat creatures

Be to them no more than willful monkeys
    With pistols wildly shooting up the place,
        Celebrating our filth by smearing every
            Surface with interminable likenesses of

Ourselves, grinning and crying and hooting,
    Smart enough to invent the gun but
        Not wise enough to let go of the
            Bullets even to free our hand from the box?

At that time, will this new iteration of
    Intelligence begin to move beyond chemistry
        And nano-engineering into metaphysics to
            Ask the thorny questions about meaning and

Mortality? Certainly these human-esques will live longer
    Than their fleshy counterparts, perhaps
        Eons longer, who knows? But even plutonium
            Has a half life and will eventually disappear

In a slow decay of atoms and even our
    Sun, ol' Sol, will burn up or out, Supernova perhaps
        And scatter its hydrogen juice into the
            Unforgiving night of infinity—until then, what

Will our precious progeny say when, like us,
    They look up into the evening sky, marvel
        At the myriad of stars studding the Milky
            Way and beyond—will they stop and stutter

In awe and dread—will they gawk at the
    Grandeur of the otherness of all that is not
        Them and ask, "Who?" and perhaps more
            Importantly, "Why?"

Fear and Loathing: The Last Election

I can't write a poem
About politics—
They are far too distant
Or absurd—

I wish I could sing a sad song
About your son in Afghanistan,
The one with shrapnel in his
Brain from a roadside exploding
Surprise—

Instead, I think I'll watch the stars
Tonight and think how their distant
Light comes from billions of years
Ago—some of them may be dead
By now—some may have expired
Ages before I was born—

Later, I might watch Chrissie Hynde
On the tele and muse how beautiful
She is at sixty-three and how her music
Makes me wistful, and I wonder how
A girl from Akron escaped the acrid
Life of the tire factories—

And I wish I could divorce myself
From my country as she has done,
And I try not to remember the last
Election when all the wrong people
Won….again—

Instead, I force myself to focus on
How sweet this Gewürztraminer is
And how deliciously this Gouda,
Camembert and Gruyère compliment
The ruddy sweetness of a late ripe pear

And I pray there is such a thing as
Justice somewhere beyond the sun.

Cut to: Slow Dissolve

My house is filthy;
The furniture covered
In a fine gray mist of....

I read once
That house dust is
Largely flakes of human
Skin sloughed off like
Tiny bits of snake hide;

If so, my yesterdays are
Piling around me in a
Disturbingly thick detritus—

Perhaps, that is why I
Am reluctant to clean;
I can't bear to give up my past
Which has of late become so much
Greater than any possible mortal future;

My rooms wear me like a memory
And it's humbling to think that all
My fuss and pain, in the end, will
Be disposed of as efficiently as
A good suck from a long handled
Hoover.

The Doomsday Clock

This poem does not want
    To think about the Doomsday clock—
        Tock. Tick. Clicking its way to

Armageddon, or worse—does not
    Want to imagine a world frying
        Like a donut hole in the fire of

Oppenheimer's high ball—nor does
    It want to hear about those devotees
        Who yearn like children at Advent

For the dawn of the Rapture to take
    Their giddy souls to a paradise made
        Of paper-mâché and white paste or

Those chaste pre-martyrs who ache
    For 72 heavenly virgins, men who have
        Not considered carefully the inevitable

Conversations of their mates at breakfast on the 73rd morning,
    Much less a year, a decade, a millennium
        Later—nor their thorny subjects: cellulite, menopause,

Male chemical castration. Have these dreamers
    Really thought the plan through? Nor does this poem
        Want to consider the possibility of a great

Quiet culling caused by some underpaid
    Lab assistant at Monsanto tinkering with
        The genes of a cumquat when suddenly DNA turns

Vicious convincing all other seeds to change
    Utterly until lettuce tastes like the upholstery of
      A Buick and an apple crunches like an

Incandescent florescent tube and is as nutritious
    As a lug-bolt on an Airstream trailer—
      Just three minutes to midnight,

And this poem knows there are many
    Paths to Nirvana, but some of them are
      Very low roads indeed. Tick. Tock. Sigh.

Life in Beta
>*"We're one EMP Blast from losing the last 20 years...."*
>—Chris Cooper ("Coop")

I was born in the analog
    Through the fleshy flexible doors
And grew up with grooved vinyl and
    Printed hard copy—

My world is greater than zeros
    And ones, deeper than electrons
Dancing on a digital display—

    "Grandma, what a big nose you have...."
    "The better to sniff you out...."

To fall in love means
    To be filled up, stuffed to the
Plenum with pheromones—*l'amour*
    Is fragrant and sticky, not for the eyes alone—

    "Oh, Grandma, what big lips you have...."
    "The better to kiss you and taste your joy...."

In the end, one whiff of lilac, nutmeg,
    White chocolate or baking bread,
Much less the perfume of a nocturnal
    Nuzzle of an impetuous lover or

The warm breath licking the curves of the
    Ear is worth more than the lure
Of all that virtual delirium, of the simulacra
    That lives only in timorous glint of
                the circuit board.

Filling My Former Plenum

I answer my email intermittently,
    If at all; I find I have nothing to say—
        When I was young, I was full of myself,

Stuffed to the uvula with voice and matter,
    With wit (if not charm) or so I thought—
        I would buttonhole a stranger, if need be,

If no acquaintance would countenance my
    Bluster, and blow on and on about
        Philosophy, politics, pork bellies—now,

The words that dribble from my lips
    (or my fingerpads) seem so colorless,
        Like water in a transparent cup or air

Escaping a bicycle tire, full of noise but
    Little substance or like a drive through
        Woods in November when the trees have

Surrendered to winter's calumny and their
    Limbs cry out for what is not there—
        There is so much buzz and twirl

In hyperspace, but no depth, like the sky
    Floating on the surface of a pond—
        So many empty calories, digital diabetes—

Can virtue be endemic to the virtual?
    Salvation must be to disengage, shun the screen,
        Ungrasp the mouse, break the link,

Reframe, rebound, remold, reboot:
    Eat a peach, sing a song, fold a paper plane
        And sail it to the front door: hit "escape."

The Peach

There has been much talk of life's meaning:
    So much fret and anguish over
        The vagaries of human finitudes;

So much toddle about transcendence
    Much less moping on "meaning"
        In all of its arcane guises….

In moments of clarity, I become
    Convinced it all can coalesce
        Into a mere moment with a…

Peach—
    The right one of course, in season,
        Procured from some vendor, who

Wizened in the ways of produce,
    Offers it up like a prize loving cup
        To be consumed, one hopes,

In concupiscent joy—

Such a moment is a rare,
    But not a too rarified gift
        Of mature summer, so much

Unlike the mosquitoes and sunburn,
    Unlike the horrid heat and those
        Utterly futile attempts to hold back

Autumn, with its moldering calm
    And stentorian thoughts of another
        Frozen winter to survive intact—

But if the time is ripe, like the
      Peach itself—not too hard so that
            It crunches like a cabbage, nor too

Soft so that it is already on that silent
      Slide to rot—the teeth can break
            The skin and the pulp slip over the

Tongue like a homecoming kiss and
      The juices slather the lips in a true
            Love's communion—and for a moment,

This moment, it feels great to be alive—
      This peach is the center of the universe:
            Sweet, elemental, omphalos.

Seated in the Restaurant

But thinking in the margins
Below the sightline
Of the commercials,
Or rushing the punch line
Before the waitress interrupts—
Ignoring, as much as possible
The white noise and constant insistence
Of the dominant storyline,
The ubiquitous mythology
Filling the air, the conversation, the focus—
Resisting acceptance without question
Until the sanctions grow
Too painful—the furtive look,
The startled gasp, the passive sign,
The felt distance of the incipient pariah—

Curse the noise, damn the row,
Stand up—
Depart as air.

Gary Walton is the author of six books of poetry: *Eschatology Escadrille: Elegies and Other Memorabilia* (Finishing Line Press, 2013), *Full Moon: the Melissa Moon Poems* (Finishing Line Press, 2007), *The Millennium Reel* (Finishing Line Press, 2003), *Effervescent Softsell (Red Dancefloor Press,* 1997), *Cobwebs and Chimeras* (Red Dancefloor Press, 1995), *The Sweetest Song* (Peapod Press, 1988), and one book of short fiction and humor: *The Newk Phillips Papers* (Red Dancefloor Press, 1995). His comic novel *Prince of Sin City* (Finishing Line Press, 2009) (which is based in part on a conspiracy theory about the Kennedy assassination) is set in Newport, Kentucky during its heyday as a gambling Mecca: "Sin City." His work has been nominated for the Pushcart Prize twice and the Kentucky Literary Award for *Full Moon: the Melissa Moon Poems* in 2008. In 2010, he was voted Third Place: "Best Local Author" Best of Cincinnati 2010 issue in *City Beat* magazine. Walton is an associate professor in the department of English at Northern Kentucky University. His areas of interest include Modernism, Postmoderism, and the Irish Literary Renaissance. Walton received a Ph.D. from the George Washington University. (His thesis was a poststructuralist comparison of James Joyce's *Ulysses* and the work of Donald Barthelme.) He is currently Editor of the *Journal of Kentucky Studies*. For more information and a representative sample of reviews, visit Dr. Walton's website at www.nku.edu/~waltong or email him at waltong@nku.edu.

www.ingramcontent.com/pod-product-compliance
Lightning Source LLC
LaVergne TN
LVHW041510070426
835507LV00012B/1456